THE ULTIMATE ANIMAL LIBRARY

Zebras

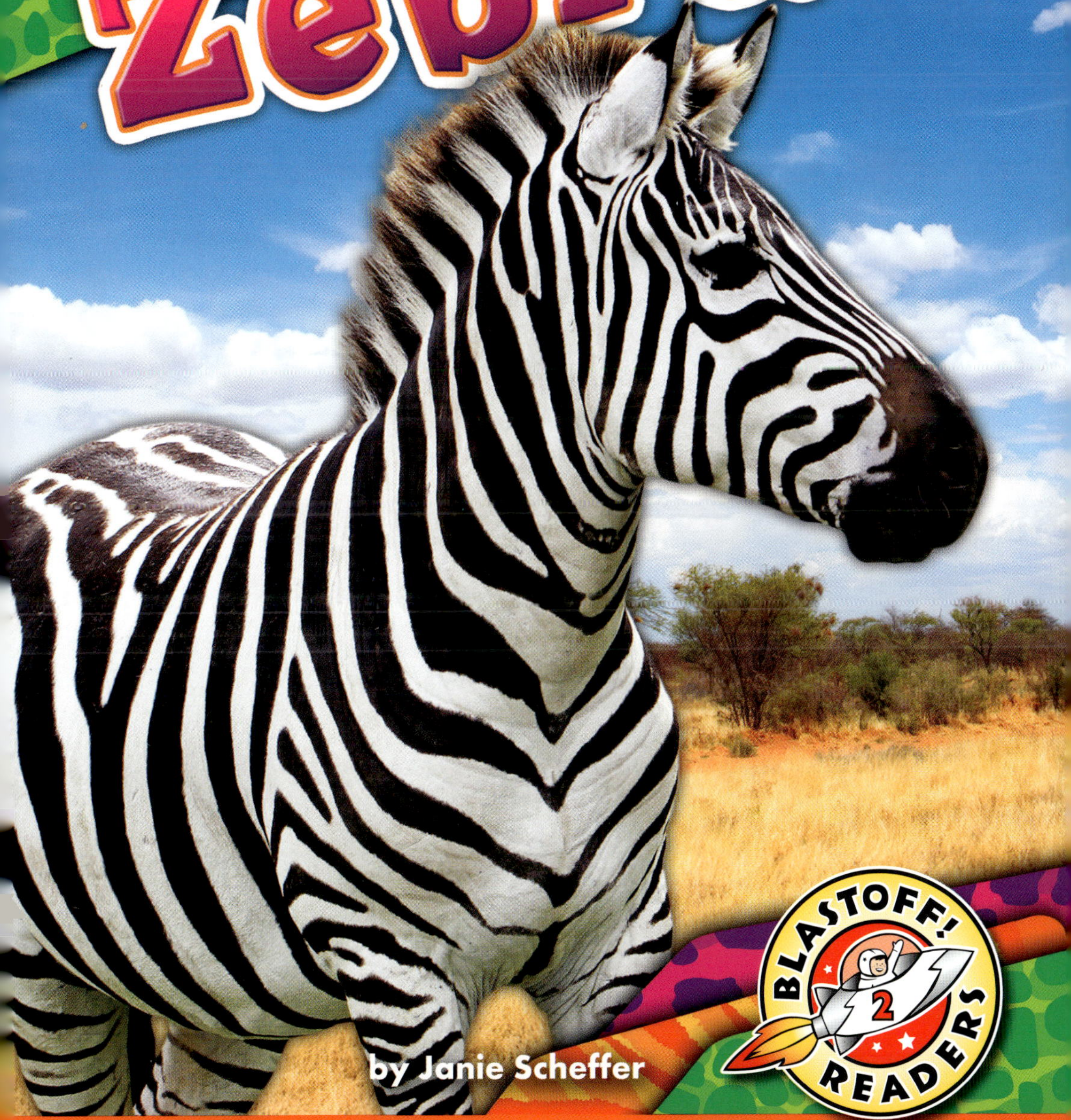

by Janie Scheffer

BLASTOFF! READERS 2

BLASTOFF! READERS, AN IMPRINT OF BELLWETHER MEDIA BY FLUTTERBEE

Blastoff! Readers are carefully developed by literacy experts to build reading stamina and move students toward fluency by combining standards-based content with developmentally appropriate text.

LEVELS

Level 1 provides the most support through repetition of high-frequency words, light text, predictable sentence patterns, and strong visual support.

Level 2 offers early readers a bit more challenge through varied sentences, increased text load, and text-supportive special features.

Level 3 advances early-fluent readers toward fluency through increased text load, less reliance on photos, advancing concepts, longer sentences, and more complex special features.

★ **Blastoff! Universe**

Reading Level

Blastoff! Beginners — Grade K

Blastoff! Readers — Grades 1–3

Blastoff! Discovery — Grade 4

This edition first published in 2027 by Bellwether Media, Inc.

Library of Congress Cataloging-in-Publication Data is available at www.loc.gov or upon request from the publisher.

ISBN: 9798898800444 (hardcover)
ISBN: 9798898801687 (ebook)

Editor: Elizabeth Neuenfeldt Designer: Brittany McIntosh

Printed in the United States of America, North Mankato, MN.

Table of Contents

What Are Zebras?

Zebras are **mammals**. They are related to donkeys and horses! They are mostly found in eastern and southern Africa.

Plains Zebra Report

Range

Status in the Wild

near threatened

Habitats

grasslands

savannas

shrublands

Zebras have striped **coats**. No two zebra coats look the same!

Their coats may make it harder for flies to bite them.

Zebras have large heads and strong necks. Their **manes** are black and white.

Their sharp front teeth chomp on grass. Their eyesight and hearing are excellent!

Zebras have long legs and tough **hooves**. These help zebras run on rocky ground.

Their hairy tails help keep flies away.

Spot a Zebra
black-and-white
mane
hairy
tail
striped
coat

Gather Around!

Most zebras live in **grasslands**. Most form small family groups.

One male leads several females and their **foals**. Family groups gather to make **herds**.

Zebras are active during the day. Most travel to find food and water.

These **herbivores** mostly eat grasses.

Zebras work together to stay safe from **predators**. They gather around mothers and foals to guard them.

Males will fight hyenas and other predators.

Growing Up

Female zebras give birth to one foal. One hour after birth, foals can run.

Foals stay close to mom. Foals learn mom's stripe patterns.

Foals drink mom's milk. After a few weeks, foals begin to eat grass.

Foals stay with mom for up to three years. They can live for up to 25 years!

Life of a Zebra

Name of Babies

foals

Number of Babies

1

Time Spent with Mom

up to 3 years

Life Span

up to 25 years

Glossary

coats—the fur or hair covering some animals

foals—baby zebras

grasslands—lands covered with grasses and other soft plants with few bushes or trees

herbivores—animals that only eat plants

herds—large groups of zebras

hooves—hard coverings on the feet of some animals

mammals—warm-blooded animals that have backbones and feed their young milk

manes—hair that grows from the necks of some animals

predators—animals that hunt other animals for food

To Learn More

AT THE LIBRARY

Chang, Kirsten. *Baby Zebra or Baby Giraffe?* Minneapolis, Minn.: Bellwether Media, 2025.

Gillespie, Katie. *Zebra.* New York, N.Y.: Lightbox Learning, 2025.

Parkin, Michelle. *A Dazzle of Zebras.* Parker, Colo.: The Child's World, 2024.

ON THE WEB

FACTSURFER

Factsurfer.com gives you a safe, fun way to find more information.

1. Go to www.factsurfer.com.

2. Enter "zebras" into the search box and click 🔍.

3. Select your book cover to see a list of related content.

Index

The images in this book are reproduced through the courtesy of: Patryk Kosmider, front cover (zebra); muratart, front cover (background), pp. 2-3; dima shiper, p. 3; pchoui, p. 4; EcoPrint, pp. 6, 15 (heyna); Nick Dale Photo, pp. 7, 15 (cheetah), 21; QUINTUS STRAUSS, p. 8; Wirestock Creators, p. 9; Sygnator, p. 10; Romas Vysniauskas, pp. 10-11; kwadrat70, p. 11; Miguel Schmitter, p. 12; knelson20, p. 13; brigetteve, pp. 14-15; Richard Juilliart, p. 15 (lion); Voodison328, p. 15 (zebra); RabbitHolePhoto, p. 15 (grass); imageBROKER.com, p. 16; Panoramic Images/ Alamy Stock Photo, p. 17; KenCanning, p. 18; Nick Dale, pp. 18-19; pruit phatsrivong, p. 20; moskha.com, p. 22.